SHE

A Sista Girls' Guide to Overcoming Her Past
& Pursuing A Limitless Future

A Sista Girls' Guide to Overcoming Her Past & Pursuing A Limitless Future

NYSHELL LAWRENCE

All scripture references are The Living Bible Translation unless otherwise noted in the text.

Printed in the United States of America.

ISBN-10: 069256960X
ISBN-13: 978-0692569603

Photography:
Images of diverse women © Dollar Photo Club in addition to personal images used with permission.

Published & Distributed By:
Jolyv Etc. Publishing

www.nyshell.com

For Joelle & Olyvia

She is clothed with strength and dignity,
and she laughs without fear of the future.

– Proverbs 31:25

CONTENTS

ACKNOWLEDGEMENTS

ACKNOWLEDGEMENTS

Thanks be to God, who always causes us to triumph! I acknowledge that I am absolutely nothing and nobody without God. He is the beginning and end to my every endeavor. I am truly thankful for the plan that He's ordained for my life and the grace He's supplied to complete it.

To my husband, Jonathan W. Lawrence, thank you for recognizing my potential and pushing me out of my comfort zone. Without you I'd still be a girl with a dream, rather than a woman with vision. I love you!

Thanks to my girls, Joelle Amaris and Olyvia Wesleigh. My greatest accomplishment will always be being your mommy. If I teach you nothing else always remember that there are no limits.

To my parents, JoEl and Marcia Watson, there aren't enough "thanks" to accurately express my gratitude. Thank you for your training, guidance, support and love. I get "it" now!

As the saying goes, "Behind every successful woman is a

tribe of other successful women who have her back."
Thank you Mariyah, Candace, Datrice, Ebony Janice, Effie,
Imoni, Ja'Nett, Latanya, LaKiesha, Latoria and Peggy for
being my tribe.

To Pastor Larry and Lady Lene'a Trice, and the entire
Tabernacle of David Church family – thanks for your
never-ending love, encouragement and support.

Pastor Emeritus Angelene Trice, thank you for speaking
into my life and being an example of wisdom and grace.

Lastly, thank you to everyone who has impacted this story.
Your positive and negative contributions have taught me
life lessons I won't soon forget and blessed me with the
opportunity to help others pursue limitless futures. It's all
good!

INTRODUCTION
"Sho' Nuff Free"

INTRODUCTION

"Sho' Nuff Free"

Rumor has it: You're kind of a big deal. No, seriously. Word on the street is, you've got some colossal ideas. Call me crazy, but I believe you have exactly what it takes to take this world by storm! Let me tell ya, your new business, is the solution everyone is looking for. The book, you have yet to publish, is dying to become a best-seller. Folks need what you've got to offer. You can't afford to procrastinate any longer. Time is of the essence. What are you waiting for?

I've been there: Staring hopelessly at my computer screen, waiting for the text to type itself. Or better yet, veggin' out on the couch watching Netflix because you have so much to do and absolutely no idea where to start. I get it. Dreams are magical. Dreams are exciting. Dreams can be exhausting. Unfortunately though, the longer you wait – to jump, to leap, to try, to fly – the longer it'll take you to get where you're going. That is, where you need to be.

I come from a family of entrepreneurs. For as long as I can remember, my parents had side gigs. The most influential though, would be the desktop publishing company that they owned. As an 'intern,' I made my first flyer for print, at the age of 10. Back then we were using Print Artist & Printshop Pro software. Trust me, we've come a long way! I've been freelance designing since 2008 and over the past several years, I've had the opportunity to work with a number of awesome clients. Professionally, there is no greater joy than knowing that I've contributed to helping someone else launch into their purpose. Whether starting a new business, publishing a book or hosting an event, the options are limitless. I'm here to help you get where you're going; creatively speaking, of course.

Bottom line: I want to see you succeed. I'm a big believer in pursuing your passions, following your dreams and living beyond limits. As a matter of fact, that's my mantra. It's the reason I exist and how I know this book, SHE: A Sista Girls' Guide To Overcoming Her Past & Pursuing A Limitless Future, will inspire you to do just that.

If ever asked to describe my life, I'd say, "It's been worth the press." While I can't testify that it has been easy, I will confess that much of my pain has been self-inflicted. I didn't sign up to be a single parent but, by choosing to have sex before marriage, ultimately I "chose" the possibility and then the actuality of that life.

Although transparent; this isn't a tell all. If you're looking for juicy gossip, honey, you won't find it here. This is a story of an overcomer. It's a tale of finding truth and walking in total victory; a declaration of freedom.

This Sista Girls' Guide has been a long time coming. I'm talking sweat, tears and many sleepless nights. I wasted plenty of years running from my purpose and avoiding my dreams. I was afraid of failing and afraid of succeeding. So essentially, I was stuck. I can't stress enough that the excerpts to follow were not written to hurt or shame anyone. One of the biggest struggles I've had with sharing my story is the realization that it won't always be pretty.

Fact: *My story is my truth. It's not always attractive, appealing or desirable but it's mine.* I'm not perfect and I never want to pretend, or lead anyone to think, that I am. Girlfriend is flawed beyond what you may care to imagine. I've got my ways. Trust me. Most days I look like I've got it all together – amazing what a coat of foundation, a dab of blush, red lips and a well put together outfit can do. Glitter ain't necessarily gold and there is much more here than what meets the eye. At first glance, you see my makeup, marriage and ministry – which, of course seems like the fairy tale life we all grew up hoping and dreaming for – but there's much more to my story.

Fact: *I've sinned. I've struggled. I've battled. I've fallen. I'm standing. I'm an overcomer.* I'm convinced that we don't struggle just for struggle's sake but we are supposed to learn from the struggle and then teach someone else. One area that many Christians have failed in is being transparent. We make it hard for new believers. We come to church on Sundays in our best apparel, driving our fancy cars, nose up in the air acting like we ain't never been through nothing. We create standards that seem impossible for a new convert to ever live up to. We pretend we were born saved, singing "Jesus I'll never forget," but the truth is we did forget. Or, again, this "forgetfulness" is a part of the act of "ain't never been through nothing."

We're married now, no need to bring up the out of wedlock child we aborted.

We've been saved 10 years, no need to mention that past drug addiction.

In no way am I suggesting we publicly air our dirty laundry to the world or cast our pearls before the swine, so to speak. But how dare we diminish God's glory and act like He didn't have to deliver us from anything? Our testimonies, no matter how great or small they may seem, have the ability to help others to overcome. It's our duty. (I'll step off my spiritual soapbox now.)

Fact: *I'm not the only one.* When we're "going through" it feels like we're all alone. Most times it seems like ain't nobody endured no suffering like the suffering we're enduring. What I've found to be true though is, just because folks aren't vocalizing their struggles doesn't mean they haven't had any. Ain't nothing new under the sun, darling!

Take me, for example – I'm not the first "church" girl to get pregnant out of wedlock and I'm sure I won't be the last. Matter of fact, it's already been proven that many would follow after me; just as I followed the ones before me. So now that I'm happy, married and sho' nuff free, I have a couple options: I can pretend like this is how life has always been and go on about my business or I can share my experience and help someone else get "sho' nuff free." It took me about 6 years to get out of the bulk of my struggle. What if my story can help the next woman get out of hers in 3 years? Or better yet, help her avoid the struggle in the first place. Yes ma'am, that's what it's all about!

There aren't enough of us pursuing our passions, following our dreams and living beyond limits – that's my 'why' and the reason behind "SHE."

As ugly as it might get, this is my truth; intended to help someone else get "sho'nuff free" with me.

THE STRUGGLE IS PART OF YOUR STORY

01.
SISTA BABY MAMA

SISTA BABY MAMA

"Congratulations, you're pregnant!"

Okay, maybe you're not but just use your imagination here and go with it. Under different circumstances that would be the best statement you've ever heard. But your situation is far from normal. Instead you're plagued with the stigma of becoming a single mother. If you're anything like me you knew the results but sheepishly lived in denial until seeking medical attention. You may have even prayed "God if you just make this go away, I promise to get it right this time!" But no, you've been exposed. Mama always said, "What's done in darkness will come to the light!" Now you know for yourself, what they mean when they say, "fat meat is greasy."

Doesn't matter if it was your first time or 30th, it only takes one time to change your life forever. This is it. If you thought life was hard before, don't expect this to be a walk in the park. When was the last time you pushed a stroller wearing 4-inch heels?! Exactly! The rules have changed.

And while I'm here to make it very clear for you that the game is much different, I also want to encourage you with the reality that it is definitely not over.

I'm sure you knew better. Maybe you were raised in the church and were provided every tool to lead a "wholesome," productive life. Yet, somewhere along the way you took a wrong turn – a detour, if you will. Or perhaps you didn't know much about holiness at all, but you saw the struggles of single mothers in your neighborhood and that, if nothing else, was a lesson that you just didn't hold fast to. Or maybe you were raised in a single parent home yourself. Whatever your introduction, at this point all of that is irrelevant. What's done is done and life goes on. What matters now is what you plan to do with the rest of your life.

You may have been told that you've ruined your future or that now you won't amount to anything; however, that's only true if you choose to believe it. That's right, it's a LIE! I've found that sometimes people who love us say things they don't truly mean in an attempt to save us from ourselves but that's a whole 'nother book, for a completely different day! Regardless of the situations we get ourselves into, God still has a plan for us!

God doesn't change his mind just because we mess up sometimes. If that were the case, He would've written me off a long time ago. Additionally, the plan God has for you, was predestined before you were even formed in your mother's womb. Think about that, God knew you were going to slip up, mess up and fall down before all of that came to pass. He said, "I know the plans I have for you." Never forget that.

May I get transparent? It's difficult being the one to bring shame upon your family. Now the whole world is looking at you cross-eyed because there's a baby growing inside of your belly. Everyone knows, before you physically start to show. You can hear the whispers before they even cross their lips: "Girllll, did you hear?! – SHE'S PREGNANT!"

Fortunately for me "pregnancy" wasn't my first dealing with "church folks." I knew them all too well, which is probably part of the reason I chose to rebel in the first place. There was one lady in particular though, who I really looked up to. She was in her late 30s, never been married, dressed to kill, she could preach her behind off and most importantly, her hair was ALWAYS laid! As a teenager I thought, "When I grow up I'ma be just like Sister Suchy-Much!" She took a liking to me as well and took on the big sister role, until it no longer looked good on her resume, it seems. Shortly after I had my daughter, I saw Sister Suchy-Much at a church meeting. I walked all the way across the sanctuary to greet her but instead of simply saying "Hello" she snarked, "I already saw yo baby!" Without comment, I returned to my seat, with my baby (insert major attitude here).

Don't expect everyone to understand your situation, especially if they've never been in your shoes. Maury Povich (and other "reality entertainment") has conditioned and encouraged us to judge, laugh at, look down on and make fun of single mothers. Quite frankly, we're portrayed as ignorant, loud-mouth sluts. And okay, yeah, sleeping with half of St. Louis is probably a really bad idea but I'd venture to say that the issue is far deeper than home girl simply can't (or won't) keep her legs closed. There's always more to the story.

Every time I see another young girl pregnant it absolutely breaks my heart. So innocent and naïve, I just want to hug her real tight and say, "Baby, you have no idea what you're about to go through!" I mean yeah it's cute now while everyone is doting over you and planning baby showers and what not. Oh, but you just wait until it's you and that baby alone struggling. Never-mind the days when money runs short or that cute kid has the nerve to ask for something you're not in a place to provide; the spiritual and emotional toll that it takes on your life alone is enough to kill you – or at least make you want to die sometimes.

In 2008 and 2009 I was afforded the opportunity to serve as leader over my church's Single Parent Ministry (SPM). Although not intended to be gender exclusive, we were a group of young single mothers, between the ages of 18-30 on a mission to redefine the single parent experience. We met monthly on a Friday night and partook in a variety of activities that were not only fun and educational, but helped us develop a "sisterhood." Through the process, we were able to be mentored by 'more seasoned' single mothers in the church – it was truly an awesome experience. Not only was I given the opportunity to teach (this responsibility forced me to avidly study the Bible) but I learned so much, naturally and spiritually, from those around me.

One of my biggest problems or hurdles with SPM was that not everyone wanted to be a part of the ministry. I couldn't understand it. We had t-shirts, tote bags and buttons. We held workshops, game nights and vent sessions – without judgment. We would even pick you up from your house, feed your family, provide childcare for your children and then take you back home. Why would anyone choose to miss out on all of that?!

There was one young lady who challenged everything we did. We had to beg her to come to events, and then pick her up because she didn't have a car. Yet, she acted as if she was doing us a favor by attending. You could tell, just by her foul attitude alone that she was struggling bad. I wanted desperately to help her but there's only so much you can do when a person is unwilling. Eventually, she stopped coming to church all together. In all honesty, I felt as though I had failed her.

Fast-forward a few years and this same individual is

beautifully saved and winning others to Christ! She doesn't even look like that same girl who would sit in my classroom with her arms folded and feet propped up on a chair. Her whole demeanor has changed; she goes out of her way to give compliments and has gone through an amazing transformation! Not too long ago she came to me and said, "I just wanted to thank you for the work you did with the Single Parent Ministry. I didn't appreciate it then but I get it now."

I'd given up on her. I had done all that I knew to do and was simply done. Fortunately God doesn't give up that easily. While I couldn't see the immediate results of SPM's impact in her life, God had a plan. Single Parent Ministry was simply a seed planted and with the help of others it has been watered and is now flourishing beautifully. God gives the increase!

Much like the Single Parent Ministry, this book is a seed. It's probably not the end-all, be-all to your existence but hopefully it will cause you to take a retrospective look within and gain insight on your life's purpose. It's my prayer that by the time you reach the last page, like that young lady, you'll be able to say "I get it!"

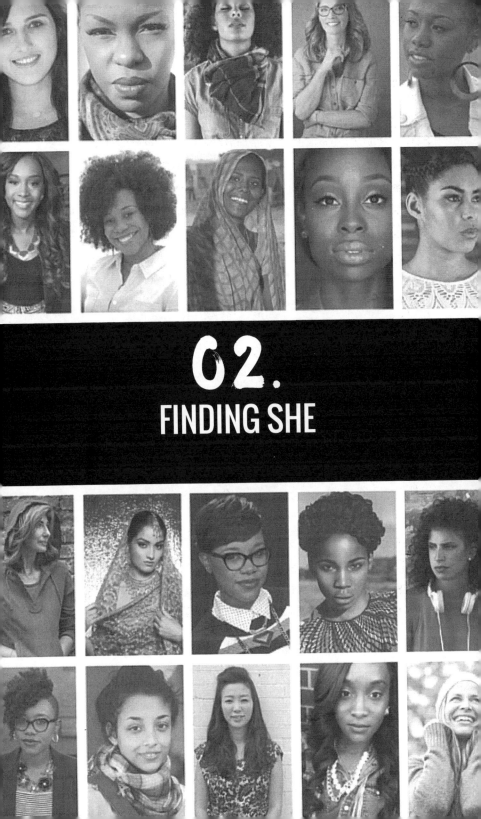

02.
FINDING SHE

FINDING SHE

Who is she? A question she'd asked herself time and time again, yet received no clear answer. While fully aware of who "they" wanted her to be, she embarked on a journey of self-discovery in an attempt to find the true definition of "she."

she/shee/
pronoun
1. the female person being discussed or last mentioned; that female.
2. the woman: she who listens learns.
3. anything considered, as by personification, to be feminine: spring, with all the memories she conjures up.

[She] is the eldest daughter of an elder and missionary; born into a family known for their pursuit of holiness and open display of excellence. She was raised up in the sanctified church – after red lipstick was no longer considered a sin, yet before preachers openly and unapologetically displayed homosexual tendencies. She

was trained to believe that "holiness is right."
"Teach a child to choose the right path, and when he is older, he will remain upon it." – Proverbs 22:6

Some of my first memories happened at church. From fluffy dresses to ruffled socks, Easter songs and Christmas speeches; it's amazing how so much of my current life reflects what I learned in the pews as a child. I gave my first speech at the age of two. My mother made sure there was a "word" in my mouth and mic in my hand as often as possible. While other children proudly exclaimed "I just came to say Happy Easter Day!" Or said, "Happy Birthday Jeebus!" I, on the other hand, was forced to learn and recite whole chapters in the Bible, beginning with John 14: "Let not your heart be troubled. You are trusting God, now trust in me. There are many homes up there where my Father lives, and I am going to prepare them for your coming. When everything is ready, then I will come and get you, so that you can always be with me where I am. If this weren't so, I would tell you plainly." – John 14:1-3

I envied the children that were allowed to giggle, play or even cry their way out of reciting their speeches. There were some kids that you just KNEW were going to clown on stage and shame their respective families. For me, that was never an option. My mom was not about to beg, plead or threaten me in front of the congregation – I already knew the deal.

In high school I ~~was forced into~~ entered my first oratory competition. I don't recall the assigned topic but it was probably something real COGIC like, "If I were State Supervisor my message to the Deaconess Missionaries would be…" Of course the answer is "holiness is right" but that's not the point of this story. Somehow, this time, I found myself totally unprepared. I stumbled over every word and struggled to remember the basic components of the full armor of God. When it was all said and done I lost. I came in third place and there were only three of us competing.

That day I learned a couple important things:
1. I'm a sore loser.
2. Success is not derived from osmosis but through hard work and preparation. You can "think you can" all you want but in order to "know you can" you have to put in some effort.

"Work hard so God can say to you, "Well done." Be a good workman, one who does not need to be ashamed when God examines your work. Know what his Word says and means." – II Timothy 2:15. I vowed to never lose another competition based on my unwillingness to prepare for the "fight." It's okay to come in third if you know you gave your all, but never because you weren't prepared. I went on to win several state competitions and even competed (and placed) nationally.

It didn't end there though. When I was sixteen, I ran for "Ms. Young Woman of Excellence" a state pageant based on an essay question and answer segment, talent presentation, interview and funds raised. Weeks before the pageant I sent a letter to our family's massive Christmas card list – inviting them to attend the pageant and of course, solicit their financial support. For weeks, my mom drilled me on current events, possible interview questions and perfecting my talent. No rest for the weary – Girlfriend was in it to win it! And that's exactly what happened, May 2002, I was crowned "Ms. Young Woman of Excellence" and declared myself unstoppable.

FAST FORWARD TO 2007

She is a single mother; a classic case of "girl meets boy and loses her darn mind." She never intended for life to turn out this way but at this point, it is what it is.

SHE IS UNSTOPPABLE

03.

SHE THAT HUNGERS

SHE THAT HUNGERS

She's hungry – this experience is more than a mere tickle in her stomach indicating that it may be close to noon. In fact, she's developed quite an appetite, accurately representing her desire for change. She is no longer satisfied with the status quo. No longer content with living beneath her means. She's irritated by her past complacency – growing tired of familiarity. She is ready; ready to embark on unchartered territory. Ready to pursue her passions, follow her dreams and live beyond any and all limits!

hun•ger/huhng-ger/
noun
1. a compelling need or desire for food.
2. the painful sensation or state of weakness caused by the need of food: to collapse from hunger.
3. a strong or compelling desire or craving: hunger for power.

This hunger is deeper than the physical sense of the word but continues to travel far beyond the depths of her soul.

There's an apparent void that can no longer be filled by the pleasures of this world. She senses that there is more to her meager existence than what she's currently experiencing. Is she perfect? No, not at all. She's been hurt, scarred and experienced great pain, but recognizes that her trials, intended to make her strong, have molded her into the person that she is today and will greatly contribute to her future success.

She is desperate – thirsty if you will. On the street this may be considered an insult as "thirsty" women are usually seen as too eager to get something they don't really need or deserve (e.g., a man, money or popularity). But there is absolutely no shame in being desperate, when you are desperate for the right things.

"Blessed are they which do hunger and thirst after righteousness: for they shall be filled." – Matthew 5:6 (KJV)

Notice how the scripture says "do hunger and thirst," it doesn't simply say "hunger and thirst" or past tense "hungered and thirsted." It says "do," which implies that this desire is continual. You're not "about to" and you didn't "used to;" either you do hunger or you don't!

I often compare myself to the prodigal son; both naturally and spiritually speaking. His story can be found in Luke 15:11-32. It's the tale of a reckless son, who thought he was grown and decided to venture out on his own without the protection of his father. He was done going to church, done following the rules and ready to live life his own way. It's really a common story, something seen in our society quite often. There's something about turning a certain age or reaching a certain status that makes us think we can make it on our own.

As the story unfolds, he quickly spends his inheritance. Soon after there was a famine in the land so he took on a job feeding slop to pigs. He was alone, broke and hungry. Out of his desperation he was willing to eat the corncobs in the pig slop, but no one would give him any. The next verse says "he came to himself." I'd like to think of this as an "appetite shift." He remembered that he came from royalty. He realized that he was living beneath his means, swallowed his pride and set out to make things right with his father. Little did he know, his dad was standing at the same road he departed from, eagerly awaiting his return.

Has your appetite shifted to the finer, more righteous, things of God? Or are you still willingly accepting the world's slop? Remember, just because you're not physically eating out of trash cans doesn't mean you're not spiritually dining with hogs! And, if that's the case, there is no need to fret. This is just as good a time as any to come to yourself and begin accepting God's best for your life.

Many of us simply don't believe that we're worthy of

anything better than what we currently have. We get so caught up in our past mistakes and present situations that we forget that God still has a plan. Truth is you don't have to be worthy (because none of us are). We just need to be willing to execute the plan that God has for us.

I'm not ashamed of my past. Never have been and I'm pretty sure I never will be. I've done some things that I'm not necessarily proud of but when it's all said and done it was those experiences that made me who I am today. It doesn't really matter what you've done in the past – Christ makes all things new! This isn't exclusive for those who've never sinned, never been disobedient or never wandered off course (mostly because that person doesn't exist). This awesome spiritual reconstruction applies to you too – no matter how jacked up your story may be!

I've always found it interesting that God can take our sins and literally throw them into the sea of forgetfulness but man will always hold you accountable for your actions – no matter how long ago it happened or how similar the situation was to their own private dealings. I mean, how can you forget the seemingly simple things that actually apply to you – like paying your phone bill on time – but the fact that I had a child out of wedlock (or whatever other gossip or drama that you've stored for table talk) is forever engraved into your memory?! Apparently this is a matter of priority. You "choose" to not let it go. I have learned that after a while, the problem no longer lies within me but with the other person. So as long as I know God has let it go and released me into freedom, I refuse to allow anyone else to hold me hostage to my past.

My life is an open book. It doesn't take a rocket scientist to figure out why I was 27, totin' around a six year old without a ring on my finger. Unfortunately though, it's hard for people to grasp that I've moved from the area of testing to the area of testimony. No longer is my head held down in shame because I "messed up." Now I have a chance to help someone else not go down the road I traveled, and it's my goal and ultimate desire to seize that opportunity.

I'm well aware that it shouldn't matter what people think or say, but let's be real, words can be much worse than sticks and stones. You'd be surprised how many times I've gone to the altar for prayer about my migraine only to return to my seat more bound than I was when I originally walked up there. It seemed like every time someone prayed for me, they ran out of things to say so they would begin reassuring me that it was okay to forgive myself for my past "mistake." And, each time I'd storm back to my seat fuming and thinking, "My child is six; get over it already!" In reality, that was just the devil trying to knock me off my square, and I use to let him do it every single time.

What's changed? After praying, crying and begging for freedom from my horrid past, I caught a glimpse of my limitless future. Along this road of discovery, I found my purpose and passion. And I've found joy in knowing that I'm pursuing the things God planned for me before the foundation of this world.

Once you discover the great things God has in store for you (and yours), you won't waste your time focusing on the past. You'll be far too busy pressing towards the mark for the prize.

A QUICK NOTE ON PRAYER

Often, I hear people say that they're not sure how to pray or they don't know what they should say to God about their individual situations and I can relate. I've found that I'm more of a "writer" than I am a "talker." For that reason, my journals are filled with prayers.

Here's what I wrote on March 4, 2009:
Lord, I'm realizing more and more, day by day that I can't make it without you. I'm so grateful for my life experiences which continue to prove that I need Jesus for myself. You've been my provider, protector, comforter and friend. You loved me when I was too ignorant to love myself and for that, I am thankful.

Thank you for sacrificing your son so I can live. Thank you for looking beyond my imperfections and embracing me in spite of. God, back then I chose to live a hard life but now I'm choosing to live for you.

No longer am I seeking your hand; I'm seeking your face. I want to know you better, know your ways and principles, know your purpose for my life. I'm confident that the thoughts you think towards me are good. You plan to prosper me and bring me to an expected end. So, no longer will I lean to my own understanding. I'm learning to trust in you so that you can fulfill your word by giving me the desires of my heart, which are the desires of your heart.

You said that if I dwell in the secret place, I'd abide under your almighty shadow. I found that secret place in worship. It's a place of honesty, healing and restoration. A place of intimacy.

I desire a closer relationship with you. Open the eyes of my understanding. Allow me to move past the flesh and operate in your spirit. I want to experience <u>Acts 2:17</u> – Pour out <u>your spirit that I may prophesy</u>, see visions and dream dreams. <u>I want to know men after their spirit and not the flesh</u>. Activate the fire within me, your Holy Ghost power, that I may do your will, walk in your wisdom and advance your kingdom.

God, I'm desperate for you. I'm lost with you and I need you now more than ever. I know that you hear my cries and I trust that you are faithful to begin the good work you began in me. I surrender.

Amen.

I understand how prayer can seem like a big, complicated ordeal. After all, we *are* talking to the Creator of the Universe about some of the biggest issues in our lives. Remember that the overall point of prayer to communicate with God. No need to get hung up on drafting some elaborate speech. Take comfort in knowing that He already knows what you need and is simply waiting for you to talk to Him about it.

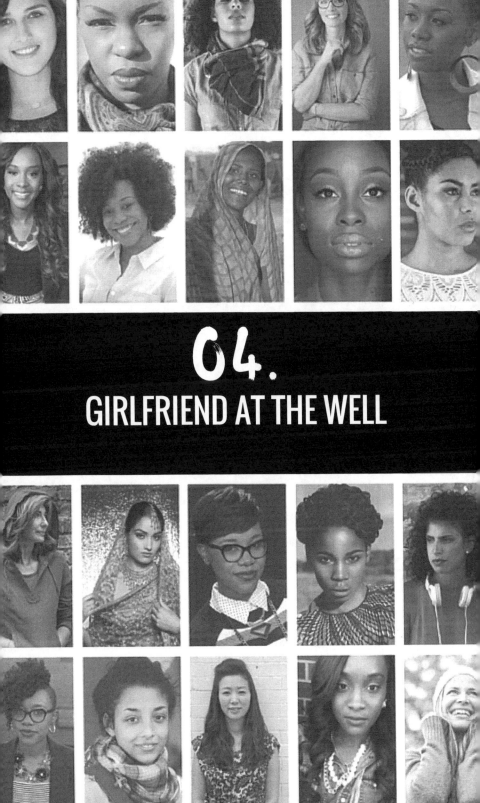

04.
GIRLFRIEND AT THE WELL

GIRLFRIEND AT THE WELL

There's a great possibility this segment should be called "Quenching the Thirst" – Either way "she" is desperate for something she hasn't yet attained. Unfortunately though, she's not sure what that "something" is, so she dibbles and dabbles in whatever she can get her hands on, in an attempt to fill the void that she feels. Some turn to drugs, alcohol or sex to escape that empty feeling. But once they've emptied the bottle, smoked up that blunt or pulled up their skirt, there is still much more to be desired.

Most times after her quest for fulfillment, she's emptier than when she started. Not only is she plagued by the original void, she is now weighed down by the guilt of sin. It's a never-ending cycle, from empty to emptier, to totally depleted.

"But whosoever drinketh of the water that I shall give him shall never thirst - but the water that I shall give him shall be in him a well of water springing up into everlasting life."
– John 4:13 (KJV)

Girlfriend was standing at that well minding her own business. As a matter of fact, for her it was just business as usual. She went to the well as she often did but this day was different. Today, Jesus, the King of the Jews, approached her, asking for water. Can you imagine? She was a Samaritan woman and the scripture tells us that Jews had no dealings with Samaritans. I'm sure she was shocked that he was even talking to her, let alone requesting a drink.

I like to imagine her rolling her neck a bit as she said, "What do you think this is? Who are you to be asking me for water?!" I bet she was all kinds of sass and attitude. Jesus' response was simple, "If you knew the gift of God, and who it is who says to you, 'give me a drink,' you would have asked him, and he would have given you living water." This scripture gives me so much life!

If you only knew the incredible things that God had in store for you, you wouldn't waste your time on things that only offer temporary fulfillment! Just in case you didn't catch it: God has incredible things in store for you so, don't waste your time on things (and people) that only offer temporary satisfaction! It's not enough to simply "press" – we have to make sure we're using that energy on things that will actually benefit us.

Whether she knew it or not, girlfriend at the well was searching for something. You don't go through THAT many men simply because you're bored. She had some deep-rooted issues. She was lonely, looking for acceptance and attempting to relieve the spiritual gnawing in the pit of her stomach with natural remedies. Little did she know the answer to all of her problems was lying in the palm of one man's hand, rather than in the bed of many men. The awesome part about this soap-opera saga is, all she had to do was ask. Girlfriend didn't have to turn a trick, sign a contract or donate any money. She asked and then she received.

"For if you tell others with your own mouth that Jesus Christ is your Lord and believe in your own heart that God has raised him from the dead, you will be saved. For it is by believing in his heart that a man becomes right with God and with his mouth he tells others of his faith, confirming his salvation. For the Scriptures tell us that no one who believes in Christ will ever be disappointed. Jew and Gentile are the same in this respect: they all have the same Lord who generously gives his riches to all those who ask him for them. Anyone who calls upon the name of the Lord will be saved." – Romans 10:9-13

Don't you want that? *Salvation. Freedom. Rest.* You can have it! It's yours for the asking.

Maybe you're having trouble relating to the woman at the well. I get it. That was back in the Bible days. You have a faucet so why would you go sit at a well and wait for Jesus? These are clearly valid points. There was a time that

I didn't know, either. I was raised in the church, given every tool needed to succeed, yet there was a period in my life where I had no idea what my purpose was. I felt a void and had no idea how to fill it. So I turned to sex and meaningless, borderline abusive relationships. I spent at least seven years walking around aimlessly searching for something more. All I found was more heartache and pain.

I visited the "well" time and time again, yet I couldn't find the remedy to quench my thirst. I'd go to the altar, fall out and roll around but by the time I returned to my seat, let alone got home, I was once again parched. Guess what? Church is not a quick fix! As my former Sunday School teacher would say, "Going to church makes you a Christian, as much as lying in a garage makes you a Cadillac!" I knew how to dress, act, talk and shout. I could "pick 'em up and put 'em down" with the best of them but I still had issues.

While going to the altar is a good step, it's only the first step. Yes, you want to be purged of everything that's not like Christ but you have to replace those negative things with positive ones. If you don't, you're in for a world of trouble! Romans 12:2 tells us, "And be not conformed to this world: but be ye transformed by the renewing of your mind..." It wasn't until I began to seek God for myself through studying the scriptures, fasting and praying that I was able to reach a point of wholeness. Am I perfect? Heck no! But I'm constantly striving for excellence, knowing that satisfaction is found in Christ rather than man.

Ugly Tendencies
There are some ugly people in this world and I'm not talking about mere physical attributes. There are just some things all the rhinoplasties this side of Beverly Hills will not fix. Ugly is as ugly does. Sorry to get all Forrest Gump on you but it's true! I'm talking about downright hateful, mean, judgmental and depressing people. They're unhappy and don't want to see others succeed. As a result, they lead miserable lives. I know because I used to be one of them.

Back when I was unaware of my purpose and destiny, I simply didn't know who I was. And because of this ignorance, I was unable to appreciate people who were already aware of their God-given purpose. Therefore subconsciously and inadvertently I hated (and hated on) those that had a better grasp on their purpose in life than I did. For some scatter-brained reason I was convinced that their beauty or success somehow took away from my good qualities. I felt that whatever they did automatically overrode what I was doing – which, at the time, was absolutely nothing.

Of note: Most "haters" have time to "hate" because they've got a lot of free time. People living in purpose, on purpose, for a particular purpose, don't have the time or the extra energy to hate on what someone else is doing because they're too busy pursuing their own passions and following their own dreams. People living in purpose are happy to see other people succeed because they know what success costs.

How can you operate in your calling if you don't know what it is? You can't! Furthermore, you can't expect to know who you are unless you know and are actively seeking God, your Creator. His agenda is the only one that matters. Believe me; I've tried fulfilling my own agenda and the agenda that others imposed on me. It always ends in disaster.

I'm sure you're thinking "Lady, I know God! I was raised in the church and..." Let me stop you right there, sweetheart. I, too, was raised in the church. I didn't just go, I was actively involved. From poofy Easter dresses and ruffled socks to the infamous wide-brim church hats – been there, done that. I come from a lineage recognized for its pursuit of holiness. Yet, I still experienced a period of my life unsure and unaware of who I truly was and what God's plan was for my life.

I sought "things," in lieu of God's Kingdom. I sought riches, instead of righteousness. I may have known His word but I refused to seek His face for myself. I went to church on Sunday and Wednesday, that should've been enough, right? WRONG! Fact is, Sunday and Wednesday wasn't enough to keep me from falling time and time again. Shoot, it wasn't even enough to make me not want to fall. I didn't desire holiness nor did I hunger for righteousness. I was ugly and ugly people are selfish.

When you're insecure, you hoard in an attempt to gain security. You may hoard compliments or even knowledge if that's what you think it will take to gain popularity and/or recognition. I dealt with low self-esteem for a really long time and it's a very ugly thing. I couldn't fix my lips to, let alone wrap my brain around, complimenting another woman because on the inside I was dying to be more like her. In my small mind I thought, "If I admit that she's beautiful, I'm admitting that I'm not." That was such a ridiculous mindset.

As a society, we've been conditioned to want whatever it is that we don't have. Fat chicks want to be skinny. Short-haired divas want long tresses. And the shy girl wants to be noticed. That's just the way it is. I'm not sure what happened to being content in whatever state we're in but I guess unfortunately, there's always more to be desired and never a moment of just simply being content with whom you are. Don't get me wrong, there's absolutely nothing wrong with self-improvement but there is everything wrong with not being able to recognize the initial good within one's self.

My weakness was a desire to fit in. I intentionally went out of my way to blend in with the crowd. I did things I didn't necessarily like or agree with in an attempt to be liked or possibly loved. I'm not talking about anything too outrageous. I haven't robbed any banks or killed anyone. But I was definitely a "lie to kick it" type of girl. I was a chameleon – willing to change how I acted, dressed and even what I said I believed in, to gain popularity. And what's funny is (well, it's funny now but it definitely wasn't then) those people that I broke my back trying to impress, didn't really care about me at all – matter of fact in retrospect, they may have even liked me more, had I simply been myself.

I used to walk through the halls of school (and church for that matter) and hear girls say "She thinks she's all that!" Little did they know, I thought I was less than "that." In order to hide my insecurities I put up a wall. What they called arrogance was an armor of protection. Head up, shoulders back and they'll never know how ugly I am. I failed to realize, my ugliness was busting at the seams and the only person who couldn't see it, was me. Forget what they told you, ignorance is not bliss!

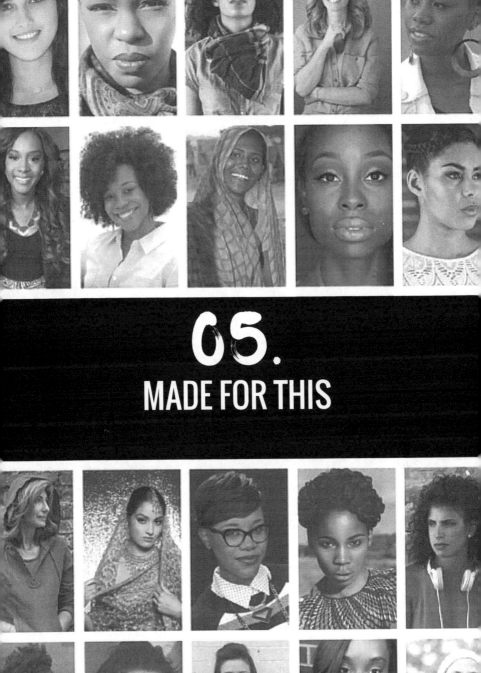

05.
MADE FOR THIS

MADE FOR THIS

Sticks and stones may break bones, but words will literally kill you. I'm not exaggerating, Proverbs 18:21 says, "Death and life [are] in the power of the tongue..." which would lead me to believe that words can be deadly. We live in a society that forces us to label everyone and everything. There are so many genres and categories – surely everyone fits in at least 1 or 2; from hip hop to country, glam to chic, emo to nerd, obese to anorexic and everything in between. Because of this mandatory labeling, it is important to know who you are, where you're going and what you're willing to accept.

You were created for greatness. Believe it or not you were. We were fearfully and wonderfully made in the image of God. Although we may have different destinies we were designed for a specific purpose. It's hard to fathom how we can all be like God yet so different. Maybe it's easier to understand if you imagine a puzzle. There are many pieces, yet one picture. Every piece is intended to fill a certain void, making each piece just as important as the next. It's not about you as an individual but about the bigger picture.

You're beautiful! I don't care what he told you or what they said. Doesn't matter what you ain't got enough of or maybe have too much of, you are absolutely stunning! Baby, you're the apple of God's eye. You are a prize to be won. Don't ever think you have to lie down, compromise or conform for a compliment. It makes no difference how much money he has or what promises he makes to you, if he loves you, he'll put a ring on it! In case you're wondering, yes I'm telling you the same things that were told to me about my worth but just because I didn't listen doesn't make them any less true. As a matter of fact, the results of my rebellion should further prove their validity.

Need a scripture? Umm, let's go with Psalms 139:14, "I will praise you; for I am fearfully and wonderfully made: marvelous are your works; and that my soul knows right well." Or we can go as far back as Genesis 1:27, "So God created man in his own image, in the image of God created he him; male and female created he them." 1 Peter 2:9 calls you "a chosen people, a royal priesthood, a holy nation, a people belonging to God, that you may declare the praises of him who called you out of darkness into his wonderful light." So like I told you, it doesn't matter what he said or what they said as long as you know who you are in Christ.

Back in the day (way back in 2005), singer Tearria Mari released a song called "No Daddy." The chorus started with

"I ain't have no daddy around when I was growing up, that's why I'm wild and don't give a f*#@!" It went on to talk about how it shouldn't be assumed that she was "givin' it up" just because she was raised in the street and her jeans fit nicely. How often do we let our situations define our actions and ultimately dictate who we become? A lot of times we hear "My dad was never around," or "My mom didn't love me like she should," and we use those unfortunate situations to justify being less than excellent, when in reality those circumstances should propel us to greatness. Seems like we'd find more pride in saying "You know what, my dad may have done me wrong but I'm going to do everything I can to make him proud anyway!" Or better yet, "I wasn't afforded certain opportunities from my parents, so I'm going to ensure that my children are given every opportunity possible to succeed." You have to be willing to press.

Fortunately for me, my dad was always around. I grew up with both parents in the home and grandparent's not far away. There was always someone telling me I was beautiful, smart and all that other good stuff. Daddy used to take me on "dates" so I'd know how a man was supposed to treat me. When I was in sixth grade we went to TGI Fridays to celebrate my birthday. I wore a green and blue plaid dress with my forest green leather coat, with the oversized hood... I was SHARP! He wore a suit, opened every door, pulled out my chair and paid for my meal – that's what a real man does.

For a long time, I blamed my failures and set backs on my father's connection to ministry. It seemed that every time I turned around he was gone on some "church business." Additionally, he's a youth advocate. So at some point or another, he was my Sunday School, Chastity Class, Children's Church and Vacation Bible School teacher. Did I mention he was ALWAYS around? Eventually, I began tuning that man completely out. To this day, I'm approached by random people claiming to be my brother, sister or cousin – meaning dad met them at the youth detention center or he facilitated their after school program and "adopted" them as a relative. Do you get where I'm going with this? I had created a story that suggested that I would need to be "troubled" to get some real attention from my dad.

Please don't get confused – In no way, shape or form am I holding anyone other than Nyshell responsible for any decisions that I've made. I did not "get pregnant" in an attempt to get anybody's attention. I'm simply showing how easy it is to blame someone else for bad choices. What does my dad have to do with this? Absolutely nothing. All of that was the "story" I was telling myself in the midst of my rebellion. My story was about me – not at all about my father.

I believe that everything happens for a reason. You can't convince me of chance, coincidence or mere happenstance – they simply do not exist. God has, and has always had, a plan. Jeremiah 29:11 says, "For I know the plans I have for you," says the Lord. "They are plans for good and not for disaster, to give you a future and a hope."

God is so intentional. Not only did He create each and every one of us as individuals made in His image and likeness, He instilled a purpose within us. He didn't make us to be idle or like dolls to place on a shelf. We were made for a specific assignment and God, being as detail oriented as He is, road mapped our lives before they even began. Jeremiah 1:5 says, "I knew you before I formed you in your mother's womb. Before you were born I set you apart and appointed you as my prophet to the nations." In other words, you were made for this.

It was never God's plan for us to struggle. In Genesis, God created Adam and then Eve. He set them up in the Garden of Eden and gave them everything they would need to survive and be successful. They had animals, fruits and veggies, they didn't even have to do laundry! But that wasn't enough for them. They went after what they thought they wanted and in turn had to suffer the consequences. As a matter of fact, we're still suffering because Eve got snaked!

How often do we go outside of God's perfect plan to get what we think we want? I can tell you first hand that it always ends up disastrous! But God, being the all-seeing, all-knowing, all-powerful, super-intelligent guy that He is, knew the decisions we'd make before we had the opportunity to make them.

I've said it before and I'll say it again: I was taught to study the Bible, fast, pray and save myself for marriage. I have no excuses to offer and no one else to blame. I see why Adam blamed Eve in the Garden of Eden. He was basically like "Lord, I know you said not to and I wouldn't have but that woman you gave me..." I'd love to place the fault on someone else but truth is I laid down what I knew, for what I thought I wanted. Case closed.

I don't know your story. But I'd admonish you to use it as a stepping stone instead of a stumbling block or resting place.

Too Hurt To Pray

Disclaimer: If you've never been "here" feel free to skip this segment as it may be hard for you to understand how one might choose to wallow in their own affliction rather than turning it over to God in prayer. Believe it or not; it happens. There have been days where I've laid in bed and cried for hours on end. I'm talking lights out, blinds closed and head buried underneath the comforter. Yet while I was convinced I was on the verge of death, not once did I ask God to help me. I knew that He could but maybe I just didn't want Him to.

06.
ON THE RUN

ON THE RUN

I remember it like it was yesterday: The moment I found out that my life was no longer my own. I'd been complaining about always being hungry, tired and thirsty. I'd missed two menstrual cycles without even noticing; figured it was just stress. This particular morning I woke up as usual, walked to the bathroom and found a pregnancy test lying on the counter accompanied by a note from my roommate, "This is yours." I was positive the result would be negative but followed through with the process just to make her happy. I peed. I waited. Soon after, I stormed into her bedroom to ask one simple question, "How many lines is this thang supposed to have?" I already knew the answer. "Mine only had one," she replied nonchalantly. "Shoot, mine has two!" I said.

Are you kidding me?! I'd just ~~run away from home~~ moved to Atlanta (from Michigan) two months prior. I didn't really have a plan. I just knew I was 20 and ready to see the world so I upped and moved. My family didn't want me to leave in the first place but I was so desperate for change, I couldn't imagine staying a second longer.

I'm sure you remember the story of the Wizard of Oz. Poor Dorothy, unhappy with her circumstances, travels to Oz in hopes of finding a remedy to her issues. I too, traveled to a land far away. Unsatisfied with my humble life in Michigan, I packed up and moved to Atlanta, Georgia – the "land of promise." Just as Dorothy woke up, realizing the whole movie was merely a dream, I was forced to wake up and face my own reality.

The first time I visited Atlanta, I looked out of the airplane's window as we were landing and the pavement sparkled. Yes, there were actual silver flecks of glitter in the cement. That was the only "sign" I needed; it was my faux yellow brick road. That day I vowed to make Atlanta my home, no matter the cost. A couple months later I found myself preparing for the big move. I'd applied for jobs and made housing arrangements with friends. I was all set. Or so I thought. Who knew that two small pink lines would change my life forever?

I called my ~~ex-boyfriend~~ baby daddy to tell him the news (read: tragedy) and he was ecstatic. I couldn't believe his excitement, considering I was scared to death. How could someone unemployed, sleeping on the couch at his mama's house, be so excited about having another mouth to feed? I know what you're thinking – If he was so *bad* what was I doing "with" him. Well, let me tell you, low self-esteem and a desire to "belong" will have you doing some desperate things. It's real easy to act out of character, when you don't know your role.

While I'm talking about him, though, let me keep it real and let you know that my situation wasn't much better. Working at Target, sleeping on a twin size mattress in my best friend's family room, while another friend slept on the couch wasn't necessarily anything to write home about. In my defense, we were preparing to move into a larger apartment but the point is at that particular moment, I had absolutely nothing to offer a child (or anyone else for that matter) and worse yet had no idea what I was going to do.

So, I did what any other self-respecting, independent, mature, grown woman would've done... I called my daddy. In all honesty, I don't remember much of the conversation. I know that he was hurt and disappointed. But in the midst of my tragic situation I recall him saying two things that have stuck with me: "If anyone can make it through this, you can!" and "If you want my help come back home." Even now I get tears in my eyes thinking about it. It was clear that my only real chance of survival was to get back under the covering of my family. So I began making preparations to return home.

The next phone call was to my Grandma. Oh to hear the pain in her voice, "I thought y'all had broke up?!" I was like, "Yeah, we did a long time ago but you know how it…" But she didn't know. She had no idea. See, she met my grandfather at a young age and he was her only boyfriend. They married when she was 16 and he's the only man that ever touched her. They had two daughters, my mom and my aunt, both of whom saved themselves for marriage – ages 22 and 29, respectively. Apparently, my genes were defective – or so I thought.

Here's the back story:
I met *him* when I was eighteen. I'd just returned home from my first year of college. Things hadn't gone as well as expected or predicted. To be honest, college was never on my "To Do List" in the first place. Since ninth grade, I'd been set on becoming a cosmetologist and began working towards that goal in high school by attending the vocational school half days. My lifelong best friend, bless her heart, convinced me at the last minute to take the ACT college entrance exam with her. I did well, applied to one school, was accepted on a full academic scholarship and that's the long and short of how I ended up a whole 45 minutes away from home.

Immediately after moving on campus, I found a student aide job in the admissions office. I soon realized that I was more interested in going to work than doing homework. It didn't take long to figure out that I would've been better off at home, in beauty school. I stuck it out for a full year and high-tailed it back home as soon as summer hit.

In my family you either work full-time, go to school full-time or work and go to school. No exceptions. So, since sitting at home surfing the internet wasn't classified as a "job," I began working at a local corner store as a cashier. You'd be surprised how many interesting people you meet while selling ice cream, liquor, cigarettes and lottery tickets.

It was July. I remember because it was extremely hot outside. Every other customer ordered ice-cream and that was my least favorite assignment. Twenty-four flavors to choose from – the only thing harder than scooping from the large cold tub of frozen deliciousness, was helping a customer decide on their flavor of the day. "Just pick one!" I wanted scream. Yep, I was miserable. This particular day was pretty normal – nothing out of the ordinary to speak of. I punched in as usual and began my duties as a cashier and fulltime ice-cream slave. I watched the customers come in and then float off on their merry way to enjoy the weather. But right before my shift was over, he walked in.

We began dating shortly after this impromptu meeting. Simple trips to the park or to the food court in the mall. He was different than any other guy I'd ever come in contact with. I met his mom. He met my parents and grandparents. He visited church with us once or twice. All was well with the world or so it seemed. I never thought to question why we rarely talked on the phone or only hung out during the day, never went to the movies together or any of that other good stuff normal couples do. It didn't seem strange that he never asked me to be his girlfriend. He called me one day after we'd been seeing each other for a couple months and told me I was his woman. I had no objections. There are at least three red flags in this paragraph alone – I chose to ignore every last one of them.

As tempting as it is to continue on with the low down on the hoedown I called love, those details are irrelevant. Transparency isn't about blaming others for foolish decisions, it's about taking responsibility for your own actions and choosing to overcome. Bottom line is: I lost myself in a relationship I had no business being in, in the first place. When I finally came to this realization it was much too late to simply walk, skip or run away. I came to a point where I was looking for the girl I used to be only to find that she was long gone. I had put on so many masks – in an attempt to find my true identity – that I became unrecognizable to myself. I looked in the mirror and hated the person I saw and despised the self-created monster I had become. I was tired – *tired of pretending, tired of compromising, tired of being talked down to and criticized, tired of going out of my way to fit in and tired of being physically used, mentally abused and mistreated.* I needed a way out.

One day while driving home from work, I began to wonder

"How fast would I need to be going to crash into a building and kill myself instantly?" I'd never thought about suicide before but that day, it was the best option I could think of. I drove a couple blocks, contemplating my own demise when suddenly I came to the realization that there was a chance I'd survive the crash if calculated incorrectly and math had never been my strong suit. I imagined myself lying in the hospital in a full body cast, wondering what I would tell my family. I couldn't imagine explaining to them that I'd attempted suicide because I wanted to get away from myself. It hurt my heart to think of the grief my untimely death would cause. So I put it out of my mind.

I sped home that day, ran to the bathroom and began to cry. Before I knew it I'd grabbed the clippers stored under the bathroom sink and shaved my head bald. Some may consider this bold step "image suicide" but it was what I thought I needed to begin my journey to self-discovery. Unfortunately, much like girlfriend at the well, I was attempting to fix a spiritual problem naturally; it never works.

I may have looked different but I was still the same weak-minded, flesh-driven, immature, insecure, little girl that I was the day before. In result I eventually did what most immature, insecure, little girls do… I ran. Have you ever tried running from yourself? Like a dog chasing its own tail – this process is exhausting and absolutely pointless.

I traveled 784 miles looking for a way out. Atlanta was supposed to be my "promised land." In reality though, it wasn't any better than the life I'd left. Oh sure, I could go wherever I wanted and return home at any time. But I found that it was hard for me to hang out late and enjoy the night life. I couldn't drink and smoke like everybody else – I talked a good game but as done as I was with God, He was only just beginning with me.

07.
RETURNING HOME

RETURNING HOME

The plan was NOT to leave in May & return in August. I didn't want a vacation, I needed a new life. So here I am, going back home for the second time, with absolutely nothing accomplished, yet again. Everyone thought I was a failure, myself included.

Returning home was much deeper than simply changing my physical address – It was truly a humbling experience. Never mind the fact that I was pregnant. It seemed like the whole world was holding up signs, saying "I TOLD YOU SO!" I had no choice but to jump off my high horse and get with the program.

When I came back to Michigan I was still on my parent's health insurance plan but that was set to expire around my due date. Upon my return, I went down to DHS, looking for help – not a handout, don't get it twisted. I was four months pregnant and jobless so, I applied for cash assistance, health insurance and the infamous food stamps. In the event that I was granted cash or food assistance I had to agree to actively search for employment and utilize the "Michigan Works!" program 20 hours per week. And since I was also seeking benefits for my unborn child, I had to agree to file for child support. The only exceptions would have been if she'd been a product of rape and/or incest. Fortunately, neither of which are part of my testimony.

The Department of Human Services represents the first time I ever truly felt ashamed about my pregnancy. I waited in the lobby for what seemed like an eternity. Finally, the case worker called my name and began to escort me back to her cubicle. Along the way I saw a familiar face – a former member of my church. "What are YOU doing here?!" she loudly exclaimed. I could feel the tears well up in my eyes and I simply replied "I'm pregnant." Now, instead of taking that time to minister to me, give me a hug or tell me everything would be just fine, she judged me. She didn't have to say a word, her facial expression spoke volumes. Apparently just that quickly, she'd forgotten that not too many years prior, she'd found herself in a similar predicament. She may be married now, but she's still a "baby mama."

Although that encounter hurt my feelings, I'm grateful that it happened. Less than 48 hours after filing my paperwork I was able to call my case worker and say "Never mind. I have two jobs now!" They were each part-time and neither provided health benefits but there was no need to continue pursuing cash assistance or food stamps.

So about these jobs... They were nothing fancy. Considering I was still living at home with my parents, they obviously didn't pay the bills. But they kept me off of public assistance and allowed me to get the necessities. I'm not even going to sit up here and play like I was so destitute. I had and still have a major support system that extends far past my immediate family. But let's be real, there's something special about not having to ask anybody for anything. And to make sure that was the case I opened at job one and closed at job two until I was physically unable to do so.

A lot of days I was unsure if I was coming or going. I'd wake up before daylight, get dressed and drive to work – stand on my feet several hours: ringing up customers, dipping ice-cream and stocking shelves. After work I'd go home and take a nap. After my nap I'd change into my second uniform, drive to work and stand on my feet several hours: helping customers, answering phones and stocking shelves. Eat, sleep and repeat.

Although, I was very grateful for both jobs, I was miserable. Every time I had to report to either job I cried like my imaginary puppy had run away and been hit by a semi-truck. I knew there was more to life than what I had going on but at this point I was simply trying to survive.

I wasn't the only one fighting for survival. See, while I was hustlin' to make ends see each other ('cuz meeting wasn't an option) *he* had the nerve to get stabbed. How selfish can you be? You mean to tell me I'm pregnant, working two jobs, so I can provide for your child and you decide to go to the club and almost lose your life over some foolishness?! Are you kidding me? Some say it was over a girl, others say he was helping someone else that was fighting about something totally unrelated to aforementioned girl – all I know is now he had a legitimate excuse not to work (rolling my eyes). So I kept pressin'.

Big Girl Panties
Be careful when accepting "help" or "advice" from well-meaning people. Seeking counsel is well and good, I encourage it, but the only way you will fully know what God has in store for you is by seeking Him for yourself. During my pregnancy I had people who were unable to have children themselves offer to adopt my unborn child. This may be a great option for some – for me it wasn't. There are consequences to everything that you do, good or bad. Had I gone this route, I'm sure I'd be the lady in prison for kidnapping my own daughter – not a good look.

I also heard "Well you know you have more options, right?" In case you didn't catch it, that's politically correct for "Just go ahead and abort it!" While I may not have had any standards when it came to sex outside of marriage, I am totally against abortion. This wasn't anything I was even willing to consider. At some point, you just have to pull up your big girl panties, swallow your pride and take responsibility for your actions.

At the age of 20, I wasn't mentally, emotionally, spiritually or financially prepared to take on the responsibility of raising a child. *I was still blowing all of my money on clothes, shoes and accessories.* Ready or not, it was time for me to grow up.

I am so thankful for my parents giving me the appropriate amount of support needed to get on my feet. I can still hear my mother saying, "This is your child. I've already raised my kids." While my parents, G-Dad & G-Ma, have always been ready, willing and available to chip in and watch their "G-Baby," it was also made clear from the beginning that she would ultimately be my responsibility.

P.U.S.H.

Ordinarily we say "P.U.S.H." stands for "Pray Until Something Happens" but in this instance it simply means PUSH!

On Wednesday, January 17, 2007, just 10 days before my 21st birthday, I gave birth to a little girl and I named her Joelle Amaris.

08.
THAT ONE DAY I SNAPPED

THAT ONE DAY I SNAPPED

"You're a bitch. Your mom's a bitch. And I'm done dealing with you." I couldn't believe he was telling me this at 6 a.m., just three months after I had his baby. And I certainly didn't think our so-called relationship could end this easily. My pastor often says "It's going to get better. If it doesn't, God will provide a way of escape for you!" And for me, this was absolutely it.

We'd spent the morning arguing on the phone about who should keep our daughter while she was sick. My choices were letting her stay with him or having my grandparents keep her, while I worked first shift. I chose my grandparents. Logic? He never had to be responsible for a well-baby, let alone a sick one. At least with my grandparents I didn't need to worry about them doing the right thing. Shoot, they helped keep ME alive all these years! Needless to say this made "baby daddy" very unhappy and we've been mortal enemies ever since. *Alright, y'all know I'm exaggerating. We're not full blown enemies but I can admit that we don't get along most days.*

See, up until this point, I did exactly what he told me to do. I was scared. No reason in particular. He yelled a lot – threw things against the wall – and well, I don't like a lot of commotion. In order to avoid the child-like temper tantrums, when he said "JUMP," I jumped – no time to ask "How high?" There was something about this day though, that wouldn't allow me to jump. Once again I was simply tired. The baby may have only been 3 months at the time but I knew that I was doing her a disservice by allowing myself to be mistreated. Let's be real, you can only bend over backwards so many times before you snap. Some may be more flexible than others. It took me three whole years to get to my absolute breaking point.

I should've caught on when I was seven months pregnant and he invited me to the movies. We drove my car because he didn't have one at the time. While in line to purchase the tickets he asked "You got this?" Trust me, he wasn't joking. Huh? Did you for real just ask me to go to the movies and then expect me to pay? Yep, sure did. The current 'me' would've left his behind standing in the middle of the cinema. Instead, I opened my wallet and obliged. Or maybe it should've been the time I showed up at his mom's house after one of my prenatal appointments only to find the barber shop chick running out of the front door. Perhaps I should've called it quits when he got stabbed or even when he threatened to knock out all of the windows in my house because I refused to take our four-week-old daughter out in the cold to visit him. For some reason though, it took him calling my mom a "bitch" to take me over the edge. *Nobody talks about my mama!*

The thing I regret most is giving her his last name. In retrospect it may appear that I simply gave up or maybe I was just too tired from fighting about everything else. But in reality, at that time, there was a piece of me that still believed that when it was all said and done, we'd end up being one big happy family – Mr., Mrs. and baby. I dreamed of the day I'd become his wife and not without merit – we spoke of marriage many times before. Yet once I became pregnant, he could no longer guarantee that we'd live happily ever after. He instead promised to always take care of our daughter and that was good enough for me.

From the moment I found out I'd be a mother I fantasized about baby names. As most mothers do, I put a lot of time, thought and energy into finding the "perfect" name for my expected bundle of joy. I brainstormed with him, friends and even searched the World Wide Web. Without knowing what she'd look like or how her presence would impact the world, I wanted her to have a name that meant something. A name she could take to the White House, if she so desired.

While realizing the importance of her first name and the effect it could have on her future, I never considered the consequences of her last. Had I known I'd be raising her without him or predicted the gruesome events that took place after her birth, I'm sure I would've given it a lot more consideration – at the very least a hyphen.

Not even 24 hours after giving birth my mom asked, "Whose last name are you giving her?" I couldn't quite wrap my mind around the reason for her questioning. He's her dad. He's claiming her. He's signing her birth certificate and affidavit of parentage. What more do you want? It didn't take long to discover that additionally I'd be wanting (and requiring) child support, responsibility and just a little bit of R-E-S-P-E-C-T. Can I get an Amen?!

09.

YOU MADE A MISTAKE;
DON'T MAKE IT A HABIT

YOU MADE A MISTAKE;
DON'T MAKE IT A HABIT

My dad's mom, Grandma Tex, is a woman of very few words but some of the best advice I've ever received came from her. She simply said, "Don't have nan 'nother one with him!" That's Camden, Alabama for "don't make the same mistake twice."

It's not my place or intention to judge but I've never understood how women have multiple kids to raise by themselves. As much as I LOVE my daughter I absolutely could not imagine starting this whole process over on my own – this is not a situation I'd like to find myself in again. Is having a child going to make you stop having sex? Probably not. But hopefully at the very least you'll think twice about your prevention methods. And hopefully, at some point, you'll realize that you deserve so much more than what you've been accepting.

It's also hard for me to understand why people would ask

me if I wanted more kids... SHOOT, can I get a man FIRST?! In the words of the Negro spiritual and Sista Maya Angelou, "I wouldn't take nothing for my journey now..." but life is hard enough as it is, let alone adding the stress of another child and possibly another baby daddy. I'm sorry but that just could not be me!

Becoming a mother doesn't make you (or require you to be) perfect. Mistakes come with the territory. But I do believe that the responsibility of parenting should motivate you to learn from said mistakes and do everything possible to avoid similar behavior in the future. Maybe you didn't know the first time; but, after time two or three you're no longer simply making mistakes, you've formed a habit and the only responsible thing to do is break it!

Avoiding the Okie-Doke
While preparing for my daughter's birth it never crossed my mind that at some point I would have to fight for her custody. Like I told you before, I always just figured at some point we'd be a real family, with the same last name. But things definitely didn't turn out that way. After the break-up, after the child support order and after a parenting time schedule had been developed, he filed for joint custody. To this day I'm not sure if it was truly because he wanted to assume half the responsibility of raising a child or if he just liked the idea of me paying child support six

months out of the year. Either way it grieved my heart.

Now you may be in your seat yelling "Bravo! It's about time men stand up and start raising their kids!" Under normal circumstances I'd be right there with you but, as always, there's more to the story.

This is probably the best time to stress the importance of waiting until you're married to have sex. On top of the risk of HIV and STDs there's DHS, FOC, PPO... maybe even CPS and believe me when I tell you, ain't none of them acronyms cute! Furthermore, you need to make sure that you are equally yoked to the person you're with. Married or not – If you go to church and he doesn't, there's going to be a problem. If he smokes marijuana and you don't, there's going to be a problem. If you work and he won't, girl, you've already got a major problem!

If you're in a situation, similar to any that I've mentioned – GET OUT WHILE YOU CAN! While I'm not a lawyer, psychologist or relationship expert, I know what it's like to be in a bogus relationship. And if I could've mustered up the same courage in 2004 that I magically developed in 2007, my life would've played out a whole lot different. I could've avoided plenty stress, heartache, and pain. Oh and let's not forget embarrassment!

Imagine being escorted to your car from the Friend of the Court (FOC) office because your child's father clowned so bad about his child support order, your caseworker feared for your safety. Or picture yourself going to the County Clerk's office to hand a member of your church, a county employee, your personal protection order (PPO) paperwork. Then on top of everything else you've endured (read: been put through), be falsely portrayed as a bad mother simply because once in your life you decide to stand up for yourself.

It would have been much more convenient to avoid the struggle and simply let the chips fall where they may. Once you become a parent though, mere convenience should no longer be the objective – especially when the well-being of your child is at hand.

To be honest, all the issues I complain about now, he had when I met him. He didn't change, I did. They say that love/lust is blind, but when I was actually able to hold my daughter in my arms, my eyes were fully opened. It was no longer about what I wanted, or what I thought would make me happy; I had a child to raise. Therefore, I could no longer listen to "I'll stop smoking next week" or "I'll look for a job tomorrow." While personally I may have been okay with the foolishness, in my heart, I knew *she* deserved much better.

Walking away wasn't the hard part, staying gone was my struggle. Don't judge me! No one in their right mind wants to raise a child alone, especially if there's a chance you may not have to.

Women are constantly accused of "trapping" men by "getting" pregnant but I'm sure you can name at least one woman that was "tricked" into her current relationship. She fell for the "okie-doke." He promised that he'd changed – now he's going to marry her, give her the moon and take her places she's never seen – and out of loneliness, desperation or perhaps pure stupidity she finds herself putting up with the same foolishness she fought so hard to be free from. No worries; it happens to the best of us, some more often than others.

Worst advice ever: "Follow your heart!" I don't know about you but my "heart" has gotten me in some pretty jacked up situations. Just as easily as lust is mistaken for love, what you assume to be your "heart's desire" could very well be your hormones. We're still keeping it real, right?! "The heart is the most deceitful thing there is and desperately wicked. No one can really know how bad it is!" – Jeremiah 17:9. Contrary to popular belief, there's no relationship worth sacrificing your self-esteem, morals or values. You think you're lonely now, try having the "title" of a relationship with no substance.

What if he changed? Girl, it's possible, but I wouldn't suggest basing that change on a visit or two to church or a sudden improvement in attitude. The fact of the matter is, only time will tell. And it's important to wait and see if this "change" is permanent before you make any life-altering decisions. This holds true to *NEW* relationships as well. It's tempting, especially as a single mother, to get on the "first train moving." Often times someone visits church one time, shows a little interest and we're ready to settle down and get married but impatience can lead to disaster. It's been my experience that many men will say what they think you want to hear – and rarely follow through. *I realize there are exceptions but I'm speaking in a generalized manner just to acknowledge the theme amongst sistas and sista friends alike who have similar, if not the same testimony. But again, I honor the exceptions.*

After the break-up I was all prepared to move on with my life. But this time I wasn't settling for less than what I deserved. This time I was going to date somebody saved and live happily ever after. The first guy to approach me was just that – I'd seen him at church a couple times in passing but we officially met at work. He was tall, semi-handsome and a fantastic singer - Most importantly though he knew the Lord. I knew this because he constantly quoted scriptures, out of context of course. Sure he was 13 years older than me, had spent a little time in jail and had two kids – but who was I to judge? Not like I wasn't a single parent myself!

After being "friends" for a few weeks, his life began to spin out of control. First his father died, and then his mother became extremely ill. As if that wasn't enough he was evicted from the house he was renting. Talk about being down on your luck! It seemed like things couldn't get any worse, until he found himself back in jail. Yep, this would totally be described as Job-like experience except for the fact he was actually driving without a license, eluding and evading police and carrying drugs with intent to sell. But he was "saved."

It is not my intention to generalize, bash or talk down about men. Simply to prove a point that we must be cautious about whom we connect ourselves to, regardless of who or what they claim to be. "A tree is identified by the kind of fruit it produces…" – Luke 6:44

JOURNAL ENTRY

I was looking for love and found its counterfeit in an unemployed, marijuana dependent, verbally abusive man. I'm sure this type of reality is usually exclusive to girls raised by single moms. Never met their dad. Molested by male figures in or out of the home. That's not my testimony. Low self-esteem is no respecter of person. It breeds insecurity. An insecure person will do whatever it takes to avoid rejection – even if it costs them their dignity. He told me I was beautiful once or twice; my father told me millions of times. For some reason though, it meant more coming from him. They say flattery gets you everywhere. I don't disagree; it's addictive.

10.
DEAR BABY DADDY

DEAR BABY DADDY

An open letter

Let's be real – Things didn't turn out the way we planned. It's a shame that an innocent child will now suffer because two adults were unable to set aside their differences long enough to consider her best interest. She deserves better but now she's stuck with a mother trying to do too much and a father not willing to do enough to make a positive impact in her life.

You claim you hate to have "the man" all up in your business, but had you been a man and handled your business from the start, going to "the man" could've easily been avoided. Yes, I too am aggravated that our parenting must be regulated by a case worker with too many cases to properly handle ours in the first place. But I guess that's what happens when two people in lust decide to play house because they're too immature to marry.

For the record, this is not about "the money." While I appreciate your monthly financial contribution, I'm not sure how much you think I can accomplish, with the little bit you're required to give. If at any point I seem bitter, just consider there's a good chance I'm sleep deprived or worried about how ends will possibly meet this time.

It's never been my intention to keep her from knowing your family and if I could change the way things went down, God knows that I would. For every action there's a reaction in an attempt to bring satisfaction to a situation too far gone. I'm willing to admit there were times that I was wrong – I'm not placing blame.

See, I've changed. It may be hard for you to recognize, but I'm not the same little girl you met working at the corner store some time back. I've grown. My focus has shifted and I'm no longer available to play the games we once played. It's really not about "us" anyway. Now is it?

I'm over the promises you failed to keep, the lies you told on me and the names you called me to my face. You stressed the point that you could never be replaced and for that I am truly grateful. Seems to me instead of worrying about who she's calling "daddy," you'd just want her to be happy and well taken care of. She is.

I propose that we move forward with the intention of doing what's best for our child. That doesn't mean that court orders will change or our relationship will become any less strained. But today, I'm choosing to forgive you – no apology required. I've carried this weight on my back and I'm tired. I've held on to this grudge to the point of physical illness. It's grown, even mutated because I was unwilling to simply let it go. Today, though, I choose to be free. And, I also humbly ask that you would forgive me. I genuinely mean that.

Respectfully,

Sista Baby Mama

Perhaps you have your own letter that needs to be written –
Here's a good place to start:

Dear _____,

_____

_____

_____

_____

_____

_____

_____

_____

_____

_____

_____

UNFORGIVENESS

A poem of sorts

Unforgiveness tried to kill me.
Yes unforgiveness, it nearly killed me.
Hurt from my past, guilt from the last time,
I messed up.
Killing me.
What she did when;
What he said over and over again –
Killing me.
They've gone on about their business,
Yet my heart struggles with forgiveness for them.
They don't deserve it.
They hurt me.
But how much more grace and mercy
Has God had towards me?
I don't deserve it.
I hurt him constantly –
Yet He looks past my past and present,
And still loves me.
Forgiven.

God, I don't want anything to come between us or hinder me from hearing your voice. I desire to live a life so connected that people see you, instead of me. I have not given myself away – not in most areas of my life. I haven't given you control or total reign. My lips profess honor but my heart is far from you. My heart is not your heart. I sincerely, desperately need you.

I know that there are issues that only you can mend. I could've been healed but I've been to arrogant, too prideful, too rebellious and unwilling to sacrifice. I've been selfish, self-righteous, self-seeking, self-dependent. God I'm sorry. This is not about me. You have a calling on my life, you have an agenda and I have been in the way. Forgive me and teach me how to forgive.

Rekindle your plan within me and reconnect our wills. Change my format to line up with yours. Whip me into shape. Prepare me for what's to come. I'm done fighting and resisting. I want all that you have for me. So, I give you all that I have. Use me for your service.

11.
IN HER FEELINGS

IN HER FEELINGS

It wasn't an accident, she simply made a mistake. Well several mistakes, but this one in particular changed her life forever. Faced with a choice to wallow in her own self-pity or surrender to the call upon her life, she chose the latter.

As the saying goes, "Hell hath no fury like a woman scorned." Generally, we reserve this quote for directly after we've been played. A guy loses interest in what we've been serving and suddenly "Hell has no fury!" It's a promise not to let his negative behavior slide and an excuse to operate solely in our feelings.

So, what does it mean to be scorned? Here, it means to be rejected in a contemptuous way. A scorned woman has been offended and hurt deeply. More than likely, she's offered some form of love and didn't receive anything in return. She may also be described as bitter. And as the quote suggests, she's meaner than hell.

Knowing that I've been hurt, disappointed and scarred in the past, I have to constantly check my motives, especially when dealing with certain people. Am I saying "no" because it's right or because I'm scorned? Is my reasoning truly in the best interest of my child or am I simply in my feelings?

I won't bother divulging how long ago I first got the idea to write this book. Just know that it's been in the works for quite some time. I will tell you though, that a big portion of the holdup was because I had to check my heart, over and over again. While writing each chapter, I had to evaluate if the details I chose to share really lined up with the originally intended mission. As I've expressed, my truth won't always be pretty. In sharing my truth though, I want to make sure that it's a tool used for freedom and not a source of bondage. Sometimes oversharing can do more harm than good and it may be in everyone's best interest to keep some things to ourselves.

Please don't misunderstand me, it's not my intention to discount your feelings. The hurt and pain is real. As Christians though, we should be operating out of love not fear or rejection.

I can't stand to see people stuck in the past. Not too long ago, I was at a restaurant that was hosting a local high school's 20-year class reunion. Imagine my surprise watching people come in with mullets and coke bottle glasses! Say what?! Mind you, this wasn't a theme party. When you heard people say, "Girl, you haven't changed a bit," you knew they weren't lying. I couldn't help but wonder though, how in the world do you let 20 whole years just pass you by? I'm a big fan of vintage clothing – give me a "pin-up girl wiggle dress" and watch me work! But for me, the key to pulling off looks from the past is the ability to mix it with more modern pieces. While I appreciate the fashion from television shows like "I Love Lucy" and "That Girl," I don't want to look like I walked off the set of a black and white film.

The past has passed for a reason; it's dead – let it go. If you're still walking around talking about what "he" did to you ten years ago, it absolutely has to end today! A lot of times we think that we're getting back at the other person by holding a grudge against them, when in reality we are allowing ourselves to be held in bondage.

bond•age/ˈbändij/
noun
1. slavery or involuntary servitude; serfdom.
2. the state of being bound by or subjected to some external power or control.

Who wants to be a slave to their past? Not me. Who wants to give someone else total control over their life? Again, I say, not me! It's time to move forward.

Furthermore, we can't allow our past to cripple or handicap us. Often times we see the glitz, glam and apparent success of others and feel like we'll never measure up. Believe me when I tell you, everyone has past indiscretions, skeletons in their closet and precious behaviors they're not proud of.

Either you can let those things stop you from fulfilling your dreams or you can allow them to catapult you into your destiny.

10 Minutes, 10 Years Ago
I was probably about 19 and I'm guessing it was a Saturday because I was at the hair salon with my mom and sister. I'm not sure who was getting their hair done or what services were being performed, oddly enough those details don't really matter. What I do remember is that Pastor Angelene was there. Sister Carolyn – *our church beautician* – had just given her a French roll and instead of waiting for her ride to come back and get her, she asked me to take her home. I remember thinking, "Out of everyone sitting in this shop, why me?!"

Now, don't get me wrong, I love me some Pastor Angelene. Back when we used to play church in the basement, and she was still First Lady Trice – she was my first pick. I'd place my chair on the side where First Ladies always sit and exclaim "yes" and "uh-huh" while my imaginary husband, the pastor, preached the word. Growing up, I thought she and her husband, the late Elder Larry Mitchell Trice, Sr., were celebrities. So now I bet you're thinking, "If she was 'all that' why didn't you want to drive her home?" Truth is, I hate driving! As a matter of fact, the only thing I hate more than driving is driving other people.

Call it what you want, there's just something about having people in the car, depending on me to get them to their destination in one piece that makes me sweat.

We got in my dad's silver Chevrolet Impala and began the 10 minute trek to her house. Another truth you should know about me is that in addition to driving, I hate talking. I say this all the time and folks are like, "No way, you get up and do your poetry so eloquently, you can't be shy." I'd much rather talk to an auditorium of 1,000 people than make small-talk with one person. Rarely, should you worry about me striking up a conversation; never going to happen. That's another issue with driving people, most times they make you talk to them and that she did. She asked me a few questions and I answered in as few words as possible.

"How's school going?"
Good.
"Are you working?"
Yes, I am.
"Oh, where at?"
QD.
"You like it?"
It's alright.

I made her work for every last detail – longest 10 minutes of my life. When we finally arrived to her house she looked at me and said, "You're going to marry a pastor." I just stared at her in disbelief. She went on to say, "You don't like to talk or be bothered with people but when you become a First Lady, you're going to have to talk to everybody. I used to be quiet, didn't really talk to people – watch what I say."

Little did Pastor Angelene know (maybe she did) I was dead-set on being with a thug. I'd been in church all my life and was simply waiting for the right opportunity to let my inner-ratchet out. Hey girl hey! French rolls and lap-hankies were cute but I was looking for mini-skirts and stilletos. I mean I was certainly saved, but not THAT saved and definitely not saved enough to marry a pastor. While I believed her to be the woman of God, and knew her long enough to recognize that God speaks to her directly, that wasn't a word I wanted to accept. Sure, pastor's wives get all the perks, wear the best clothes and have women tripping over each other trying to serve them. However, as an outsider, I can tell you there's much more to it than looking pretty and planning Women's Day activities. Again, why me?

At this point I was already smitten with "future baby daddy" and would've married him, had he ever asked properly. Better yet, had he asked before the baby was born and all the drama popped off. So yeah, I'd definitely be divorced by now – or worse. Since then, I've had at least a couple men tell me that God told them that I was their wife. Sir, really? Is that the best pickup line you could conjure up? One, let's call him Leon, went as far as to tell me that if

I ever married anyone else I'd be committing adultery because God had already reserved me for him. No, Leon is not a pastor.

I'm married now. Truth be told, getting married had been on my personal agenda for quite some time. It bothers me though that people (in general) tend to believe (and have the nerve to express) that now that I'm married, I am in turn successful. While it is true that success is measured differently for each individual, in my case marriage is only the tip of the iceberg.

Contrary to popular belief, marriage alone will not fix your situation. If you were a mess to begin with, marriage will make you a mess with a man. And, if you refuse to get your life in order, you'll end up a divorced mess. Marriage won't make you any happier, any less depressed, or any more fulfilled than you were before the wedding day. Marriage doesn't magically erase your past and give you a fresh start. If you're looking for a fresh start – try Jesus. No man can do for you what He can. If you're looking for financial gain, then maybe marrying someone rich can solve that. If you're tired of sleeping alone, then maybe a man can give you pleasure. I can guarantee though, those solutions are short term. We're talking about heart and mind issues here, not "quick fixes." A quick fix is a hurried repair – it's "for the time being" and never meant to be a permanent solution. You're worth so much more than that!

I am so glad that my past has absolutely nothing to do with my future. Yes, I realize I've said this at least a couple times already but it's kind of a big deal and I really want you to get it. You messed up? So what! Repent and do better next time. Let me tell you, when I got pregnant at 20, plenty folks wrote me off. They said I had ruined my life and wouldn't amount to anything. No one cared about Pastor Angelene's prophecy or any other prophecy I'd received confirming my future success in life. All they knew was that I got myself pregnant. Fast-forward eight years: I'm married with two kids, serving God, appear to be doing well and most of those aforementioned folks are singing my praises. Sad part is, I haven't really done anything yet – at least not when compared to the things I plan to do over the next few years; let alone the rest of my life. God has a plan and I've only scratched the surface.

"I'm not saying that I have this all together, that I have it made. But I am well on my way, reaching out for Christ, who has so wondrously reached out for me. Friends, don't get me wrong: By no means do I count myself an expert in all of this, but I've got my eye on the goal, where God is beckoning us onward to Jesus. I'm off and running, and I'm not turning back." – Philippians 3:12-14

Imagine if I had listened to those awful, "judgy" people; I could've missed out on the promising future that God had already predestined for me! I wish you could see these tears in my eyes. When I think about what my life could have been, where I could have ended up, how my story could have concluded – and to think that despite my constant rebellion God still loved me enough to spare me and allow me to continue on with His perfect plan! It is only because of His grace. Everywhere I go and in everything I do I'm talking about pursuing passions, following dreams and living beyond limits – It's the core of my message because I remember back in 2010, when I was going through one of my go-throughs, and the only thing that kept me sane was my passion to create. I wrote poetry, painted canvas and made jewelry as if my life depended on it. And in a way it did. Girlfriend, there is no reason or viable excuse for you to be anything other than who and what God called you to. Period. You are more than capable. I meant everything that I said in the introduction of this book – I want to see you succeed. What's it going to take for you to get there?

In 2010, I suffered the breakup of all breakups. Greater than when my high school sweetheart cheated, greater than the baby daddy turning on me, greater than ol' boy going to jail.... This was something major. Never had I experienced a hurt quite like this. He and I went to the same church so, I walked around with a smile on my face and made sure I spoke real big when I saw him. Everyone commented on how "well I was handling it" and "mature I was being." We'd been dating, long distance mainly, for about two years – he was supposed to be the one. Regardless of how good I may have looked, girlfriend was tore up!

Needless to say, my journal was full of tear stains and "Lord, I can't believe he did me like that…" For at least a couple weeks, I cried behind closed doors telling sweet baby Jesus how we were supposed to get married and how bad my feelings were hurt. Maybe if I were prettier, or smarter, or if my booty was bigger… hold it! Maybe, if I'd spent as much time in God's face as I did trying to be up in the boyfriend's face, I could've avoided the whole predicament to begin with. Point well taken.

God began to show me that I'd once again lost myself "man pleasing." Just because this particular man happened to be saved, my participation in the relationship wasn't any healthier than the previous disaster with Baby Daddy. This relationship meant everything to me – I spent all of my time and energy being the best girlfriend that I could. In doing so, I neglected the fact that my calling was much greater than mastering the art of being a good girlfriend. For 24 years, I had been pursuing the wrong things – trying to become rather than simply being.

Never would I have imagined that nearly 10 years after my conversation with Pastor Angelene, I'd be married to the youth pastor at our church, the same guy that broke my heart in 2010 – funny how things work out. I had to learn that everything happens according to God's will and everything intended to happen will happen when it's supposed to. Although I believed that Jonathan was my husband in 2008 we absolutely had to take a break in 2010.

It was necessary for us to mature as individuals before we could be successful as a couple. Before I could move forward and be anybody's wife, I had to get myself together.

BLESSED IS SHE WHO HAS BELIEVED THAT THE LORD WOULD FULFILL HIS PROMISES TO HER

Luke 1:45, NIV

12.
WORTH THE PRESS

WORTH THE PRESS

Most days it seems like it's just one thing after another. Every time she turns around something else goes wrong. There's not enough money in the bank. More than likely her rent is late. And her baby daddy is cutting up like only "he" knows how.

She's fasted. Yes, she's also prayed. But she's still only hanging on by a thread. No longer living freely, she's barely surviving. What's a girl to do?

I've been there too many times to name. As a matter of fact as you're reading this there's a very good chance I'm at this point again. It just seems to come with the territory. There's a lot this girl could do, but there's one thing she's not going to do:

SHE'S NOT GIVING UP!

That's right; she's staying in the press.

Don't get me wrong, she wants to quit. I imagine her being

just one late notice, one overdraft fee or one senseless argument away from throwing in the towel. But she's aware that she may also be one step away from the blessing, breakthrough and deliverance she's been patiently waiting on. She's been through too much, endured too much, put up with too much to turn back now.

"Daughter, be of good comfort - thy faith hath made thee whole. And the woman was made whole from that hour." – Matthew 9:22 (KJV)

When you press, you push against something. It means to use a steady and significant force to put weight on something, sometimes to make it move or start working.

You may be pressed for time, have a pressing issue or even in the press.

In case you haven't heard (or noticed), I'm a hair person. Long or short, wig or extension, human or synthetic... I like my hair. So, when I think about a press, I automatically think about using a hot comb. A hot comb (also known as pressing comb or straightening comb) is a metal comb that when heated is used to straighten coarse hair and create a smoother hair texture. Heat straightens hair by breaking up the bonds that make hair wavy or curly. Although heat is important, it isn't the only factor when it comes to pressing hair. The straightness also depends on the weight and tension applied while using the hot comb.

One disadvantage about pressed hair though, the results aren't permanent. Water, sweat or any type of moisture acts as kryptonite and causes the hair to revert back to its original curly state – which means at some point, you're probably going to need to press it again. Now depending on the thickness and length of one's hair this can be a long, tiring process. But once it's over and you have your desired style, you realize it was worth the press!

I remember as a child, sitting in the kitchen waiting less than patiently as my Grandma pressed my hair. She would take the pressing comb and put it on the hot stove. She'd wait a little bit, then pick up the comb and blow it. Sometimes she'd touch it lightly with her hand to make sure the temperature was okay – she'd then apply it to my hair, and comb through with much tension. The objective was not to get burned, but sometimes it happened. Maybe on my ear, or neck or forehead – and I would cry. If you've never had your hair pressed you may be thinking "who in their right mind would sit through that torture?!" But I did, and many of us do because we want to swing our hair. We know the end result is worth the initial discomfort. We know it's worth the press!

One of my favorite Bible stories is about the woman with the issue of blood. Matthew 9:20-22 says, "And, behold, a woman, which was diseased with an issue of blood twelve years, came behind him, and touched the hem of his garment: For she said within herself, If I may but touch his garment, I shall be whole. But Jesus turned him about, and when he saw her, he said, Daughter, be of good comfort; thy faith hath made thee whole. And the woman was made whole from that hour." Short, sweet and to the point.

I'm sure this woman was tired. Just as we often are. Can you imagine the disappointment of 12 years of tests, copays and trial and error medications with no signs of relief? I'm sure she was frustrated. I can imagine her saying "You know what?! I'm done. Forget these tests and these doctors!" Just as we often say in relation to ministry: "Forget this fasting and this corporate prayer and forget what Pastor said... I'm through!"

Not so fast Sista Girl! Just think about what would've happened if this woman in Matthew had quit. She would've missed out on Christ's virtue for her life. She knew it was worth the press!

Paul said in Corinthians 3:14 – "I press toward the mark for the prize of the high calling of God in Christ Jesus." One translation says, "I keep pursuing the goal to win the prize of God's Heavenly call..." which lets us know this may not be an overnight thing. It is going to require a continual and persistent pressing.

She could've easily said after year one or two, let alone year 12, "I'll probably have this condition forever, I'm done trying." She could've heard Jesus was in town and decided to take a nap. Or she could've said, "Oh well, I'll catch him on the way back," but she didn't. She chose to press again, even though she'd been pressing for the last 12 years. She understood that her press was a process and although she was healed "suddenly" that time, she had 12 years of times where it didn't come so easily.

This Christian lifestyle is not easy. Many times we trick ourselves into believing that life is supposed to be perfect simply because we surrendered to God. Pay your tithes, give your offering and join the usher board if you want a carefree life. Reality Check: It doesn't work like that! Let's not get it twisted, all those things are good. Jesus is and always will be the best thing that ever happened to you. But going to the altar one or two times is not going to make every bad or uncomfortable thing magically disappear.

"And let us not get tired of doing what is right, for after a while we will reap a harvest of blessing if we don't get discouraged and give up." – Galatians 6:9

One problem is we don't want to go through anything. We, as a society, are very fortunate people. We rarely live uncomfortable lives and when a problem does arise we're usually able to find a quick fix. But what happens when the "fix" isn't so quick? When the going gets tough do we run away or stand firm on our faith, believing that we'll reap a reward in due season as long as we don't faint?

Unfortunate things happen but Romans 5:3-5 tells us "…we also glory in tribulations, knowing that tribulation produces perseverance; and perseverance, character; and character, hope. Now hope does not disappoint, because the love of God has been poured out in our hearts by the Holy Spirit who was given to us." Can't you see it? That trial you thought was going to kill you has actually made you stronger! It's worth the press!

I'm not going to pretend like I wake up every day ready to conquer the world – no ma'am! Catch me too early on a Monday and you'll wonder what happened to "Ms. Overcome & Pursue," for sure! I do, however, wake up each day knowing that I'm purposed to inspire someone, regardless of what I happen to be going through at the moment. In the words of Mindy Kaling: "Sometimes you just have to put on lip gloss and pretend to be psyched." (Fake it 'til you make it, darling!)

Here's what keeps me pressing:
(In addition to the scriptures sprinkled throughout the previous text)

"This is the day the Lord has made. We will rejoice and be glad in it." – Psalm 118:24

"If you cling to your life, you will lose it; but if you give it up for me, you will save it." – Matthew 10:39

"But they that wait upon the Lord shall renew their strength. They shall mount up with wings like eagles; they shall run, and not be weary; they shall walk, and not faint."
– Isaiah 40:31

"But these things I plan won't happen right away. Slowly, steadily, surely, the time approaches when the vision will be fulfilled. If it seems slow, do not despair, for these things will surely come to pass. Just be patient! They will not be overdue a single day!" – Habakuk 2:3

"And here is how to measure it – the greatest love is shown when a person lays down his life for his friends;"
– John 15:13

"Dear brothers, is your life full of difficulties and temptations? Then be happy, for when the way is rough, your patience has a chance to grow. So let it grow, and don't try to squirm out of your problems. For when your patience is finally in full bloom, then you will be ready for anything, strong in character, full and complete."
– James 1:2-4

"And we know that all that happens to us is working for our good if we love God and are fitting into his plans."
– Romans 8:28

"Now glory be to God, who by his mighty power at work

within us is able to do far more than we would ever dare to ask or even dream of—infinitely beyond our highest prayers, desires, thoughts, or hopes." – Ephesians 3:20

"These trials are only to test your faith, to see whether or not it is strong and pure. It is being tested as fire tests gold and purifies it—and your faith is far more precious to God than mere gold; so if your faith remains strong after being tried in the test tube of fiery trials, it will bring you much praise and glory and honor on the day of his return."
– 1 Peter 1:7

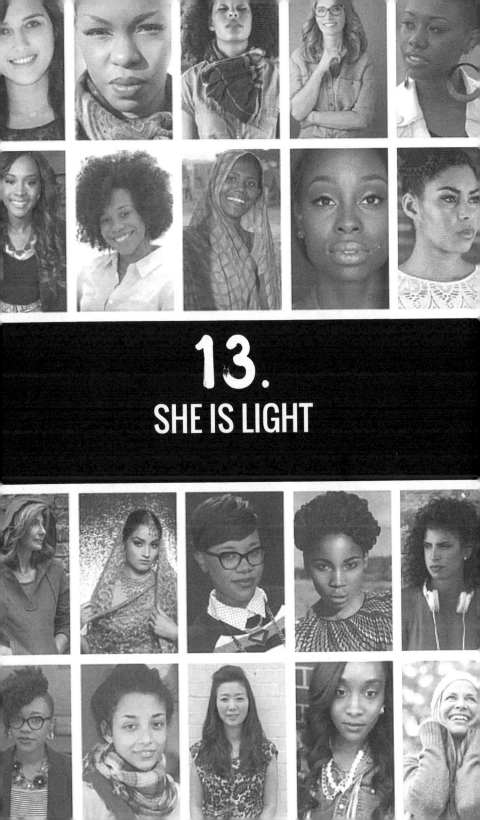

13.
SHE IS LIGHT

SHE IS LIGHT

Often times we end up in less than ideal situations and feel like it's the end of the world. Too many times, I've personally been in positions that I thought would surely take me out. But guess what? I'm still here! Girl, YOU are still here! And while we're here let's be determined to do and be what God predestined for us. You have to realize that you are greater than your circumstances. I can encourage, compliment and prod you but at the end of the day, you have to absolutely know this for yourself. You are so much more than anything you've ever been through. Forget what *he* told you or what *she* may have said behind your back. This is your opportunity to prove them wrong! The only way you'll be able to do that, is to spend time finding out what God's plan is for you and then pursue your passions, follow your dreams and live beyond limits.

pas·sion \ˈpa-shən
noun
1. a strong feeling of enthusiasm or excitement for something or about doing something.

What do you like to do? What are you good at? What comes naturally? What do you find yourself doing when you're procrastinating? What calms you down? What relieves your stress? What brings you joy? Girl why are you still reading? You should be writing this stuff down – It's time to learn about you!

_____

_____

_____

_____

_____

_____

_____

_____

_____

_____

In my own reflecting, I found that I love to design. Graphic, interior, event – doesn't really matter. I'm a natural at developing attractive color schemes, pulling elements together cohesively, creating aesthetically pleasing spaces and the like. When I should be working, I'm creating images and layouts that I may or may not ever have use for. I've never been through anything that a quick trip to the local craft store can't relieve. I eat, sleep and breathe art and creativity. And now, there is no greater joy than knowing that I've contributed to helping someone else launch into their purpose – creatively speaking of course.

Getting pregnant and becoming a 'baby mama' at the age of 20 was a definite limitation. Let's face it, the struggle is real. That could have been the end of my story. And, my tombstone could've easily read, "So-n-so's Baby Mama. The End." Fortunately, God's plan is much bigger than the limits we place on ourselves (and place on others, for that matter). Our mistakes and bad decisions don't define who we are.

According to Romans 8:1, "there is now no condemnation awaiting those who belong to Christ Jesus." Zero. Zilch. None. Once we repent (ask for forgiveness and turn away from sin), we have a clean slate with God. Again, man will always hold you accountable, but ultimately we're only seeking God's approval.

Today is not the day to give up. You have so much to live

for. There's too much left for you to accomplish to even fathom throwing in the towel now. Too many people waiting on you to succeed in order to prove to them that they have a fighting chance. Regardless of what you're going through, you better believe it's worth the press! God is with you, darling—be the light!

Don't hide your light! Let it shine for all - let your good deeds glow for all to see, so that they will praise your heavenly Father.
– Matthew 5:16

A QUICK NOTE

"Think like a queen. A queen is not afraid to fail.
Failure is another stepping stone to greatness."
— Oprah Winfrey

I can see the queen in you. Beyond the scars, hurt, disappointment and shame, reigns a queen. Regardless of what you've been through, you can walk with your head held high knowing that you were created for something extraordinary.

Don't be afraid to abandon your past (or current) and embrace the limitless future that God has in store for you. Pursue your passions, follow your dreams and live beyond limits. I believe in you!

WHAT SHE TACKLES SHE CONQUERS

RICHARD GILMORE

⌄

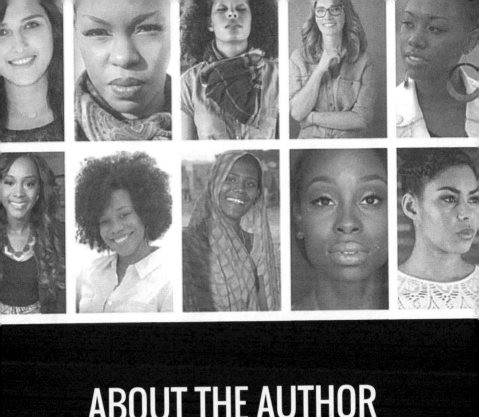

ABOUT THE AUTHOR
Meet Nyshell

Hi, I'm Nyshell

AUTHOR, POET +
VISUAL BRAND STYLIST

As an author, poet and visual brand stylist, I empower multi-passionate women to pursue their passions, follow their dreams and live beyond limits. I'm committed to helping women get unstuck and relentlessly go after the life God predestined for them. **Bottom line: I want to see you succeed!**

I'd love for you to visit me online at www.nyshell.com, where I blog about my journey through marriage, motherhood and ministry. I believe that everyone has a story and can't wait to connect with you to hear yours!

Until next time,
Nyshell

@iamnyshell

I DIDN'T KNOW WHAT I WANTED TO DO, BUT I ALWAYS KNEW THE WOMAN I WANTED TO BE

DIANE VON FURSTENBERG

NYSHELL'S BIO

It wasn't an accident, she simply made a mistake. Well several mistakes, but this one in particular changed her life forever. Faced with a choice to wallow in her own self-pity or surrender to the call upon her life, she chose the latter.

Nyshell Lawrence made her public speaking debut at an early age. Born and raised in Lansing, MI; she quickly developed a passion for art. She is a young, talented, risk-taker whose mission is to impact the world through her artistry. She's a big believer in pursuing passions, following dreams and living beyond limits. As a matter of fact, that's her mantra. It's the reason she exists and she wants you to be inspired to do the same.

From single mom to wife and creative entrepreneur, Nyshell transparently shares her journey from tragedy to triumph and passionately delivers the uncompromised gospel, through the art of performance poetry. She is the author of Scarred: The Beauty In My Pain, an inspirational collection of poems originally published in 2012.

Nyshell is the Founder of Nyshell & Co., LLC, a visual branding and design studio. As a visual brand stylist she empowers multi-passionate women in business to pursue limitless futures.

She is happily married to Jonathan W. Lawrence; together they have two daughters, Joelle Amaris and Olyvia Wesleigh. As a family, they serve at Tabernacle of David Church under the leadership of Pastor Larry M. Trice, Jr.

Her work is transparent, transformative, honest and real. Be a part of the movement SHE is "Nyshell."

THE LAWRENCE FAMILY
Jonathan, Nyshell, Joelle + Olyvia